MW01226768

Rocking Dog Between Door

by

Loretta Adu

DORRANCE
PUBLISHING CO
EST. 1920
PITTSBURGH, PENNSYLVANIA 15238

Dorrance Publishing Co
585 Alpha Drive
Pittsburgh, PA 15238
Visit our website at *www.dorrancebookstore.com*

ISBN: 978-1-6495-7064-2
eISBN: 978-1-6495-7004-8

Rocking Dog Between Door

by

Loretta Adu

Rocking dog between door.

Beaten so bad that it couldn't find it good.

What a troublemaker?

I just hate you getting hurt, crazy one.

I made you full to bite that
little one in the box.

Whoops, whoops, whoops.

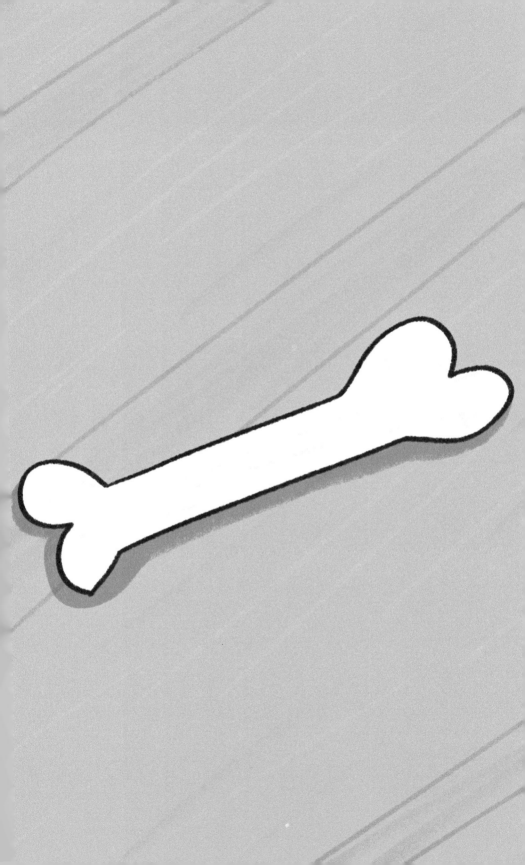

They are all crazy for one bone.

Why don't you stay at the door to
find your game?

Bye-bye, I hate you now.

You got what you got.